Especially

G000292727

From

....

Date

....

© 2013 by Wanda E. Brunstetter and Richard Brunstetter

ISBN 978-1-62416-682-2

All rights reserved. No part of this publication may be reproduced or transmitted for commercial purposes, except for brief quotations in printed reviews, without written permission of the publisher.

All scripture quotations are taken from the King James Version of the Bible.

Cover and Interior Photography by Richard Brunstetter.

Published by Barbour Publishing, Inc., P.O. Box 719, Uhrichsville, Ohio 44683, www.barbourbooks.com

Our mission is to publish and distribute inspirational products offering exceptional value and biblical encouragement to the masses.

Member of the
Evangelical Christian
Publishers Association

Printed in China.

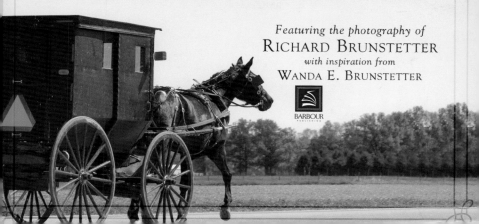

The Simple Life

365 Days of Inspiration from Amish Country

Featuring the photography of
RICHARD BRUNSTETTER
with inspiration from
WANDA E. BRUNSTETTER

BARBOUR
PUBLISHING

JULY 2

Heavenly Father, thank You for who
You are and for all that You do.
May I sense Your presence
as I worship You. *Amen.*

JULY 1

"Love your neighbor as yourself,"
The Bible says to do.
If we truly love ourselves,
Then we'll love our neighbors, too.

JULY 3

God often chooses to turn obstacles into opportunities.

JUNE 30

Trust God.
He will always provide.

JULY 4

There is freedom in doing just what God
asks you to do.

JUNE 29

A true friend is like a good book;
the inside is better than the cover.

PROVERB

JULY 5

*Trust in the LORD with all thine heart;
and lean not unto thine own understanding.*

PROVERBS 3:5

JUNE 28

Heavenly Father, help me to love others so they can see You living in me. *Amen.*

JULY 6

Let us run with patience the race that is set before us.

HEBREWS 12:1

JUNE 27

Imagine how different our world would be
if everyone loved God and their fellow humans.

JULY 7

Teach me thy way, O LORD,
and lead me in a plain path.

PSALM 27:11

JUNE 26

The grass may be greener on the other
side of the fence,
but it's just as hard to mow.

A PROVERB

JULY 8

*And my people shall be satisfied
with my goodness, saith the* Lord.

Jeremiah 31:14

JUNE 25

*In thee, O L*ORD*, do I put my trust:*
let me never be put to confusion.

PSALM 71:1

JULY 9

Instead of criticizing, choose to be an encourager.

JUNE 24

Marvellous are thy works; and that my soul knoweth right well.
PSALM 139:14

JULY 10

When you feel you have nothing left,
remember: GOD IS ENOUGH!

JUNE 23

* * *

We should be thankful for the
abundance that is ours,
For the beauty of this world, the sun,
the moon, the stars.
For our family, friends,
and God's everlasting love,
We should give thanks to
the Father above.

JULY 11

*Then shall the trees of the wood sing out
at the presence of the LORD.*

1 CHRONICLES 16:33

JUNE 22

A smile is contagious.
Share a smile with someone today.

JULY 12

And be at peace among yourselves.

1 THESSALONIANS 5:13

JUNE 21

Be ye therefore followers of God, as dear children.
EPHESIANS 5:1

JULY 13

Heavenly Father, as I go about my work this week,
help me remember to do all of it as if it's just for You.
Amen.

JUNE 20

What characteristic makes a great leader?
The ability to follow.

JULY 14

Never be afraid to let your
light shine for Jesus.

JUNE 19

When God wants to bless you,
He often does it through another human being.

JULY 15

True friends are like diamonds—precious but rare.

UNKNOWN

JUNE 18

The flowers of all the tomorrows
are in the seeds of today.

A PROVERB

JULY 16

Be ye strong therefore,
and let not your hands be weak:
for your work shall be rewarded.

2 CHRONICLES 15:7

JUNE 17

Both a person's character and
garden reflect the amount of weeding that
was done during the growing season.

JULY 17

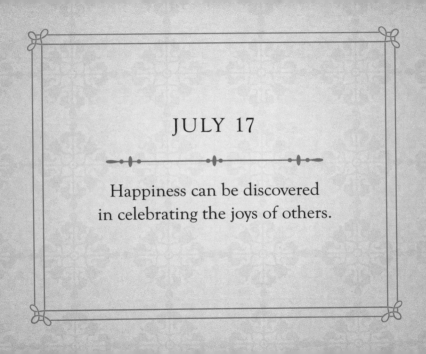

Happiness can be discovered
in celebrating the joys of others.

JUNE 16

---

*But my God shall supply all your need
according to his riches in glory by Christ Jesus.*

PHILIPPIANS 4:19

JULY 18

Let all your things be done with charity.
1 Corinthians 16:14

JUNE 15

If God be for us, who can be against us?
ROMANS 8:31

JULY 19

Seek to follow the Lord,
and always be on the lookout for ways
to help a neighbor.

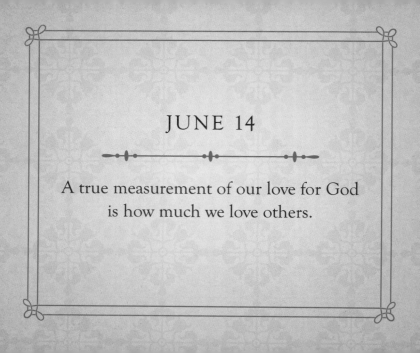

JUNE 14

A true measurement of our love for God
is how much we love others.

JULY 20

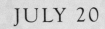

Every child of God—
including, and especially, YOU—
has a special place in His plan.

JUNE 13

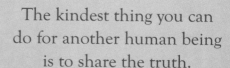

The kindest thing you can
do for another human being
is to share the truth.

JULY 21

Pray without ceasing,
for God is always listening.

JUNE 12

Keep your head and heart in the right direction
and your feet will follow.

JULY 22

Real love is helping others without thinking about
if and when they will return the favor.

JUNE 11

With good will doing service,
as to the Lord, and not to men.

EPHESIANS 6:7

JULY 23

Hope is a lot like sunshine. . . .
Sometimes it shines brightly.
Sometimes it's hidden behind
a cloud or two.
But you know it's always there.

JUNE 10

And when ye stand praying, forgive,
if ye have ought against any.

MARK 11:25

JULY 24

You're never far from a miracle.

JUNE 9

Loving others should be our aim,
Sharing and caring are one and the same.

JULY 25

Thou shalt love thy neighbour as thyself.

ROMANS 13:9

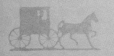

JUNE 8

God painted the sky for all to behold
So that His glory could surely be told.
There's always something
positive to be found,
For the miracles of God's
handiwork abound.

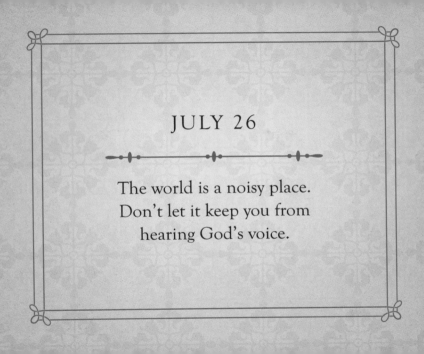

JULY 26

The world is a noisy place.
Don't let it keep you from
hearing God's voice.

JUNE 7

God has blessed us in such a way
that we can pass His blessings on to others.

JULY 27

Your expression is the most important
accessory you own.

JUNE 6

Your heavenly Father longs to spend time with YOU!

JULY 28

Then was our mouth filled with laughter,
and our tongue with singing.

PSALM 126:2

JUNE 5

*Salt is good: but if the salt have lost his savour,
wherewith shall it be seasoned?*

Luke 14:34

JULY 29

Character is measured by what we do
when no one is looking.

JUNE 4

Do something kind for someone today;
Show your love in a special way.

JULY 30

Heavenly Father, lead me in a plain,
simple path that focuses on You.

JUNE 3

The solutions to all your problems can be found
in God and His Word.

JULY 31

The simple life reminds us
that there is always satisfaction and joy
to be found in the uncomplicated.

JUNE 2

⸺•⸺◆⸺•⸺

For we walk by faith, not by sight.

2 Corinthians 5:7

AUGUST 1

A happy home is not merely having
a roof over your head
but having a foundation under your feet.

JUNE 1

Just as a flower reaches for the sun,
we should reach out to God and let
His Son bathe our souls.

AUGUST 2

I need to relax and have a responsibility to rest,
For God loves me, and He knows what's best.

MAY 31

Instead of worrying about having the best of everything,
ask God to help you make the best of everything you have.

AUGUST 3

Children's children are the crown of old men;
and the glory of children are their fathers.

PROVERBS 17:6

MAY 30

Apply thine heart unto instruction,
and thine ears to the words of knowledge.

PROVERBS 23:12

AUGUST 4

Like the garden of the LORD;
joy and gladness shall be found therein.

ISAIAH 51:3

MAY 29

More important than trying to
keep up with the neighbors?
How about taking the time to
find out where they're going?

AUGUST 5

A man's heart deviseth his way:
but the LORD directeth his steps.

PROVERBS 16:9

MAY 28

Your neighbors will always welcome a timely good deed.

AUGUST 6

Heavenly Father, remind me regularly that I need to rest in You. *Amen.*

MAY 27

❦

*And all thy children shall be taught of the LORD;
and great shall be the peace of thy children.*

ISAIAH 54:13

AUGUST 7

And thou shalt be like a watered garden,
and like a spring of water,
whose waters fail not.

ISAIAH 58:11

MAY 26

Always take time to rest and renew your spirit.

AUGUST 8

Happiness is like a butterfly,
flitting from flower to flower.

MAY 25

A calm mind and a confident heart are
available to every believer.

AUGUST 9

Be kind to your friends;
if it weren't for them, you'd be a total stranger.

UNKNOWN

MAY 24

Rejoicing in hope;
patient in tribulation;
continuing instant in prayer.

ROMANS 12:12

AUGUST 10

I will meditate in thy precepts,
and have respect unto thy ways.

Psalm 119:15

MAY 23

An attitude of trust
Is what every Christian needs.
Trust God fully,
And follow wherever He leads.

AUGUST 11

Many hands are a blessing,
for they make work seem light.

MAY 22

Train up a child in the way he should go:
and when he is old, he will not depart from it.

Proverbs 22:6

AUGUST 12

Behold, what manner of love the
Father hath bestowed upon us,
that we should be called the sons of God.

1 John 3:1

MAY 21

Our loving heavenly Father
promises to be with us—
every minute of every day.

AUGUST 13

Don't hurry, don't worry;
Do your best, and leave the rest.

MAY 20

•━•┅•━━━•┅•━━━•┅•━•

Christians are like bits of coal;
together they radiate heat and light,
but apart they grow cold and dim.

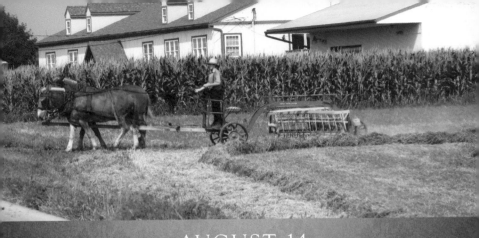

AUGUST 14

Serve him with a perfect heart and with a willing mind.
1 Chronicles 28:9

MAY 19

The temperature of your spirit
determines what grows within your heart.

AUGUST 15

Everything we have comes from God,
and He wants us to share.

MAY 18

The heavenly Father has ownership
of everything; we are mere stewards.

AUGUST 16

—•••—   —•••—   —•••—

The secret of true and
lasting peace is to give every anxious
thought and care to God.

MAY 17

Happiness can be found all along the path of life.

AUGUST 17

Heavenly Father, guide and direct me so that the things
I do are pleasing in Your sight. *Amen.*

MAY 16

God didn't create us to handle life without Him.

AUGUST 18

—•━━•━━•━━•━━•—

Favour is deceitful, and beauty is vain:
but a woman that feareth the LORD,
she shall be praised.

PROVERBS 31:30

MAY 15

I will instruct thee and teach thee
in the way which thou shalt go:
I will guide thee with mine eye.

PSALM 32:8

AUGUST 19

Wisdom is knowing what's really
important in life,
and understanding that some
things really don't matter.

MAY 14

A forever friend is a wonderful gift from God.

AUGUST 20

Fellowship builds people up and binds them together.

MAY 13

True humility credits God for every success.

AUGUST 21

The heavenly Father's arms never grow weary
of holding His beloved children.

MAY 12

A friend is someone who knows
the song in your heart
and can sing it back to you
when you have forgotten the words.

UNKNOWN

AUGUST 22

* ⋅ ❖ ⋅ * ⋅ ❖ ⋅ * ⋅ ❖ ⋅ *

Blessed is every one that feareth the LORD;
that walketh in his ways.

PSALM 128:1

MAY 11

Our greatest privilege is to enjoy Christ's presence.

AUGUST 23

Don't overlook life's small joys
because you're too busy searching for the big ones.

MAY 10

A house is built by human hands;
a home is created by the hearts that dwell therein.

AUGUST 24

How much better off we'd be if we learned
to listen to God's still small voice, instead of trying
to do things our own way.

MAY 9

He maketh me to lie down in green pastures:
he leadeth me beside the still waters.

PSALM 23:2

AUGUST 25

---

*I will praise thee; for I am fearfully
and wonderfully made.*

PSALM 139:14

MAY 8

*Let your speech be always with grace,
seasoned with salt, that ye may know
how ye ought to answer every man.*

Colossians 4:6

AUGUST 26

Live each day as though it's your last.

MAY 7

God sometimes chooses to grow
our faith through trials.

AUGUST 27

The things I can see
help me to trust God
for those things I cannot see.

MAY 6

No man has ever injured his eyesight
by looking on the bright side of things.

A PROVERB

AUGUST 28

Each person is a unique expression
of God's loving design.

UNKNOWN

MAY 5

He which soweth sparingly
shall reap also sparingly;
and he which soweth bountifully
shall reap also bountifully.

2 CORINTHIANS 9:6

AUGUST 29

Never fail to teach a child the way of truth.

MAY 4

God loveth a cheerful giver.

2 Corinthians 9:7

AUGUST 30

There's no telling how far a kind word,
or look, or deed will travel.

UNKNOWN

MAY 3

—••—••—••—

When we look around at the
beauty God created
and find joy in being with those we love,
our discontent fades,
and appreciation sets in.

AUGUST 31

Behold, I am the LORD, the God of all flesh:
is there any thing too hard for me?

JEREMIAH 32:27

MAY 2

The desire of a man is his kindness.

Proverbs 19:22

SEPTEMBER 1

In life, the test often comes before the lesson.

MAY 1

If you plant the seeds,
God will take care of the harvest.

SEPTEMBER 2

We are saved that we might serve;
but we never serve that we might get saved.

APRIL 30

Heavenly Father, remind me to appreciate
the things You've given me;
and no matter what's going on in
the world around me,
help me to learn to be content. *Amen.*

SEPTEMBER 3

* * *

A merry heart doeth good like a medicine:
but a broken spirit drieth the bones.

PROVERBS 17:22

APRIL 29

When you help someone up a hill,
you're that much closer to the top yourself.

SEPTEMBER 4

Thy word is truth.

JOHN 17:17

APRIL 28

But we will give ourselves continually to prayer,
and to the ministry of the word.

ACTS 6:4

SEPTEMBER 5

The LORD hath done great things for us;
whereof we are glad.

PSALM 126:3

APRIL 27

Bear ye one another's burdens,
and so fulfil the law of Christ.

GALATIANS 6:2

SEPTEMBER 6

A faithful life leads to a fruitful harvest.

APRIL 26

He who has a right to boast doesn't need to.

A Proverb

SEPTEMBER 7

Happy hearts make happy homes.

APRIL 25

Prayer is the bridge that carries you
from panic to peace.

SEPTEMBER 8

Wisdom is never found in a pride-filled heart.

APRIL 24

I will praise thee, O LORD, with my whole heart;
I will shew forth all thy marvellous works.

PSALM 9:1

SEPTEMBER 9

---

*One God and Father of all, who is above all,
and through all, and in you all.*

EPHESIANS 4:6

APRIL 23

Our Father cares for the birds of the air,
And He cares for us when we offer a prayer.
He provides for the birds with insects and seeds;
He provides for His children's daily needs.

SEPTEMBER 10

Life is but one continuous course of instruction.

APRIL 22

A contented heart will help you to enjoy
the scenery along life's little detours.

SEPTEMBER 11

God is never too busy to hear our prayers.
No matter the situation, He always cares.

APRIL 21

If your harvest tools are ready,
God will provide work for you to do.

SEPTEMBER 12

As we have therefore opportunity,
let us do good unto all men.

GALATIANS 6:10

APRIL 20

You are the seed that determines
the harvest around you.

SEPTEMBER 13

There is no greater knowledge
than the knowledge of Christ.

APRIL 19

Your productivity is directly dependent
on the environment you create.

SEPTEMBER 14

If any of you lack wisdom, let him ask of God.

JAMES 1:5

APRIL 18

The LORD seeth not as man seeth;
for man looketh on the outward appearance,
but the LORD looketh on the heart.

1 SAMUEL 16:7

SEPTEMBER 15

❖━•━❖━•━❖━•━❖

When worry knocks at the door,
send faith to answer it.
You'll find no one there.

APRIL 17

Commitment is dedication to something
you know God would have you do.

SEPTEMBER 16

It's not who we are but *whose* we are
that creates our happiness.

APRIL 16

A change in behavior first
begins with a change of heart.

SEPTEMBER 17

Love. Kindness. Help. Support.
All are at the heart of true Christianity.

APRIL 15

And whatsoever ye do, do it heartily,
as to the Lord, and not unto men.

COLOSSIANS 3:23

SEPTEMBER 18

Choose a job you love and you'll never
have to work a day in your life.

A PROVERB

APRIL 14

When your trust is in God,
He will often lead you in a way you don't expect.

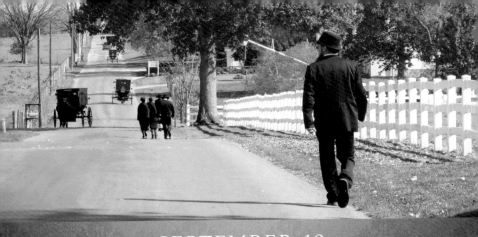

SEPTEMBER 19

I press toward the mark for the prize of the
high calling of God in Christ Jesus.

PHILIPPIANS 3:14

APRIL 13

The best hand to hold is God's hand.
He will help you walk through anything.

SEPTEMBER 20

Setting a good example for others to see,
Caring about them and not always me.
If we let our light shine by doing good deeds,
The Gospel will be spread with the sowing of seeds.

APRIL 12

Pleasant words are as an honeycomb,
sweet to the soul, and health to the bones.

PROVERBS 16:24

SEPTEMBER 21

❦

Remember as you go about
your day that you may be the only Jesus
some of your friends,
neighbors, and family will ever see.

APRIL 11

The best form of spiritual exercise
is to touch the floor regularly with your knees.

UNKNOWN

SEPTEMBER 22

Happiness is the fine art of making a beautiful bouquet
from only those flowers in reach.

APRIL 10

Cultivate a teachable spirit.

SEPTEMBER 23

And be renewed in the spirit of your mind.

EPHESIANS 4:23

APRIL 9

Leave the past where it belongs—
which is in the past.
Instead, look forward to the amazing
future God has in store for you.

SEPTEMBER 24

It's comforting to know
that God keeps the earth rotating
and the seasons changing.
He makes the sun rise every morning
and sets the sun at the
right time each evening.

APRIL 8

Commit thy works unto the LORD,
and thy thoughts shall be established.

PROVERBS 16:3

SEPTEMBER 25

There is no teaching as powerful as example.

APRIL 7

Daily fellowship with the heavenly Father
is the secret to a fruitful life.

SEPTEMBER 26

Peace is more than the absence of conflict;
peace is the presence of God.

UNKNOWN

APRIL 6

Go about your daily tasks
as though you are doing
each and every thing for the Lord.

SEPTEMBER 27

He who thinks he is
leading and has no followers
is only taking a walk.

UNKNOWN

APRIL 5

A good humor is a healing balm
for the heart and soul.

SEPTEMBER 28

God has an eraser that's big enough to
take care of all your mistakes.

APRIL 4

Truth is the most powerful thing on earth;
nothing, no matter how strong, can change it.

SEPTEMBER 29

Even a child is known by his doings,
whether his work be pure, and whether it be right.

PROVERBS 20:11

APRIL 3

For the LORD *thy God is with thee whithersoever thou goest.*

JOSHUA 1:9

SEPTEMBER 30

The more you read the Bible,
the more you'll love its Author.

APRIL 2

—•——•——•—

Heavenly Father, sometimes when
I'm feeling stressed or in a hurry,
I run out of patience. Help me remember in such
times to take a deep breath, say a prayer,
and wait patiently for answers. *Amen.*

OCTOBER 1

We ought to obey God rather than men.

ACTS 5:29

APRIL 1

In order to be what God created us to be,
we need each other!

OCTOBER 2

The measure of a man is not how tall he is,
but how much his neighbors respect him.

UNKNOWN

MARCH 31

If at first you do succeed,
give credit to the heavenly Father!

OCTOBER 3

✦ ─ ✦ ─ ✦

Value your neighbors, friends, family—
and even strangers—
more than all the riches in the world.

MARCH 30

For my strength is made perfect in weakness.

2 CORINTHIANS 12:9

OCTOBER 4

Open your heart and let God renew your spirit
as you determine to follow Him all your days.

MARCH 29

God's strength is made evident in our weakness.

OCTOBER 5

Life without Christ is a hopeless end;
with Christ it's an endless hope.

UNKNOWN

MARCH 28

—◆—◆—◆—

The nature of a flower is to wait
patiently for spring.
Flowers don't worry or complain
about every little thing.
The nature of a flower is an example to all.
When wind and rain threaten,
a flower stands straight and tall.

OCTOBER 6

The seasons come and go,
but God never changes.

MARCH 27

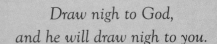

Draw nigh to God,
and he will draw nigh to you.

JAMES 4:8

OCTOBER 7

My sheep hear my voice, and I know them,
and they follow me.
JOHN 10:27

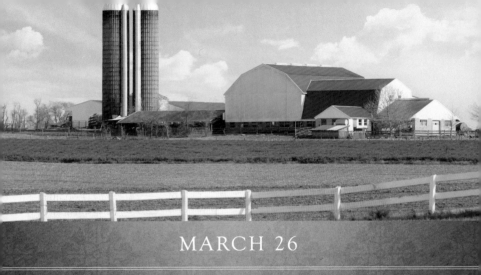

MARCH 26

Give, and it shall be given unto you.

LUKE 6:38

OCTOBER 8

Come unto me,
all ye that labour and are heavy laden,
and I will give you rest.

MATTHEW 11:28

MARCH 25

Look not every man on his own things,
but every man also on the things of others.

PHILIPPIANS 2:4

OCTOBER 9

Yesterday is gone; tomorrow is uncertain;
today is here, so use it wisely.

U<small>NKNOWN</small>

MARCH 24

Christian hospitality is an open heart
and an open home.

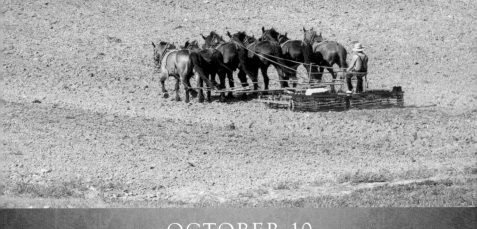

OCTOBER 10

The Christian life is about becoming
rich in relationship with the Lord.

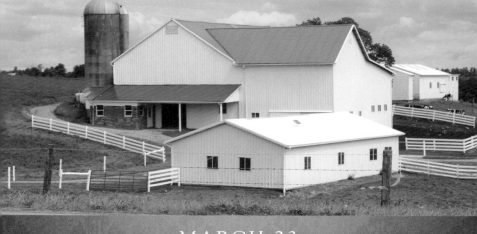

MARCH 23

Faith is believing the Lord will do
just what He says He will do.

OCTOBER 11

When you forget yourself,
you usually start doing something
others will remember.

UNKNOWN

MARCH 22

The only people who never fail
are those who never try.

OCTOBER 12

*Whoso findeth a wife findeth a good thing,
and obtaineth favour of the LORD.*

PROVERBS 18:22

MARCH 21

The LORD is good,
a strong hold in the day of trouble;
and he knoweth them that trust in him.

NAHUM 1:7

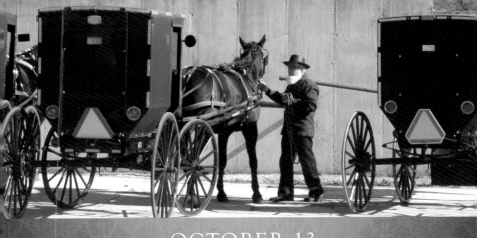

OCTOBER 13

God often works through us to meet
the needs of those around us.

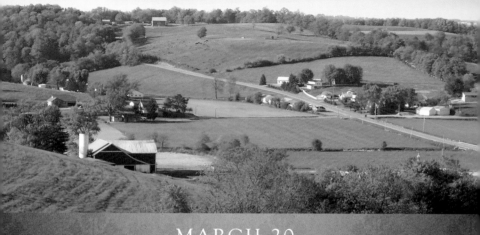

MARCH 20

When you're fearful,
lay your worries at God's feet.

OCTOBER 14

Heavenly Father, show me how I can best serve
You in ways that will help others in my community.
May Your love and generosity be shown through me.

Amen.

MARCH 19

The act of giving is a vivid reminder
that it's all about God, not us.

OCTOBER 15

Reach up as far as you can,
and God will reach down the rest of the way.

UNKNOWN

MARCH 18

Never say "never";
never say "always";
and never give up.

OCTOBER 16

Weave in faith, and God will find the thread.

UNKNOWN

MARCH 17

Exercising your faith daily
is the key to godly character.

OCTOBER 17

The LORD is my light and my salvation;
whom shall I fear?

PSALM 27:1

MARCH 16

Remember the sabbath day,
to keep it holy.

Exodus 20:8

OCTOBER 18

Doing a good deed in secret
gives an added blessing.

MARCH 15

Home is the "first school" and the "first church"
in which children learn about God's love.

OCTOBER 19

God is only a prayer away.

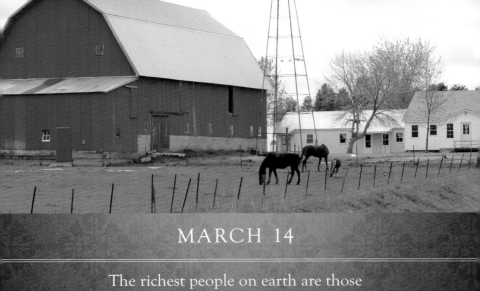

MARCH 14

The richest people on earth are those
who invest their lives in heaven.

OCTOBER 20

The earth is full of the goodness of the Lord.

PSALM 33:5

MARCH 13

Looking for ways to serve others
is pleasing to God.

OCTOBER 21

For we are made partakers of Christ,
if we hold the beginning of our confidence
stedfast unto the end.

HEBREWS 3:14

MARCH 12

*Let the beauty of the L*ORD *our God be upon us.*

PSALM 90:17

OCTOBER 22

The Lord of hosts is with us.
Psalm 46:7

MARCH 11

The straight and narrow way has the lowest accident rate.

A PROVERB

OCTOBER 23

The Bible is like a compass;
if you follow where it points,
you can rest assured you're
going in the right direction.

MARCH 10

You can't see around the corners;
but be thankful that God can.

OCTOBER 24

*Come ye yourselves apart into a desert place,
and rest a while.*

MARK 6:31

MARCH 9

Remember that a joyful heart is
pleasing to the Lord,
and it's an added benefit to know that
it's good for you, too!

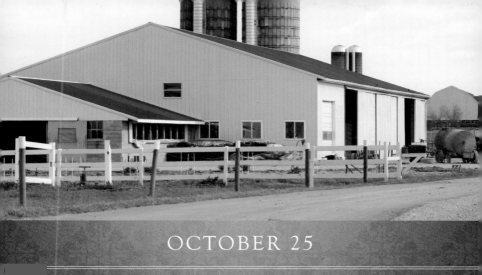

OCTOBER 25

If you don't cut the peace pattern just right,
you'll only have scraps.

MARCH 8

The path of your life will change each time
you determine to hold fast to your faith.

OCTOBER 26

*Whosoever therefore shall humble
himself as this little child,
the same is greatest in the kingdom of heaven.*

MATTHEW 18:4

MARCH 7

For where two or three are gathered
together in my name,
there am I in the midst of them.

MATTHEW 18:20

OCTOBER 27

Rejoice in the Lord always:
and again I say, Rejoice.

PHILIPPIANS 4:4

MARCH 6

How excellent is thy lovingkindness, O God!

PSALM 36:7

OCTOBER 28

Our ray of light is Jesus!

MARCH 5

New reasons to praise the Lord
present themselves each day!

OCTOBER 29

When you keep your eyes on Jesus,
everything comes into focus.

MARCH 4

*Yea, all of you be subject one to another,
and be clothed with humility.*

1 Peter 5:5

OCTOBER 30

———•◦•——— ———•◦•——— ———•◦•———

But they that wait upon the LORD
shall renew their strength.

ISAIAH 40:31

MARCH 3

Always look forward
to what God has in store for you tomorrow.
Each new day is a gift!

OCTOBER 31

Confidence in the presence of God is where
you will always find comfort.

MARCH 2

For ye shall go out with joy, and be led forth with peace.

ISAIAH 55:12

NOVEMBER 1

*That I may publish with the voice of thanksgiving,
and tell of all thy wondrous works.*

PSALM 26:7

MARCH 1

Heavenly Father, remind me to look
at the brighter side of life.
Thank You for the gift of laughter.
Help me to use it often.
Amen.

NOVEMBER 2

*In whose hand is the soul of every living thing,
and the breath of all mankind.*

JOB 12:10

FEBRUARY 28

Our greatest hope on earth is help from God above.

NOVEMBER 3

Spend some quiet time in the presence of God.
Simply being with Him will refresh your spirit.

FEBRUARY 27

When a man's ways please the LORD,
he maketh even his enemies to be at peace with him.

PROVERBS 16:7

NOVEMBER 4

Our main interest in this world should
be to secure an interest in spending eternity
in the presence of our Creator.

FEBRUARY 26

You can't store up treasures
in heaven if you're holding on
to the treasures of earth.

NOVEMBER 5

Read God's Word with an open heart;
then pray about the message
your heart receives.

FEBRUARY 25

Let every thing that hath breath praise the LORD.

PSALM 150:6

NOVEMBER 6

It's never a waste of time when you're waiting on God.

FEBRUARY 24

For the eyes of the Lord are over the righteous,
and his ears are open unto their prayers.

1 PETER 3:12

NOVEMBER 7

But as for me and my house,
we will serve the LORD.

JOSHUA 24:15

FEBRUARY 23

This is the day which the L ORD *hath made;*
we will rejoice and be glad in it.

P SALM 118:24

NOVEMBER 8

Prove all things;
hold fast that which is good.

1 Thessalonians 5:21

FEBRUARY 22

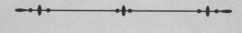

If you honor God in your heart,
He will be honored by your life.

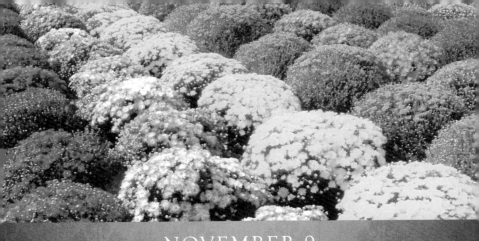

NOVEMBER 9

Let God control you on the inside
and you'll be genuine on the outside.

FEBRUARY 21

I can do all things through Christ which strengtheneth me.
PHILIPPIANS 4:13

NOVEMBER 10

And on the seventh day
God ended his work which he had made.

GENESIS 2:2

FEBRUARY 20

Truly the light is sweet,
and a pleasant thing it is for
the eyes to behold the sun.

ECCLESIASTES 11:7

NOVEMBER 11

There's a lot to be thankful for
if you only take the time
to look for life's little blessings.

FEBRUARY 19

Being obedient to God's commands
is the goal of life's journey.

NOVEMBER 12

What you think about most determines your character.

FEBRUARY 18

A sign of true contentment?
Accepting the bitter with the sweet.

NOVEMBER 13

Christ, the Rock, brings hope to a hopeless world.

FEBRUARY 17

Take therefore no thought for the morrow:
for the morrow shall take thought
for the things of itself.

MATTHEW 6:34

NOVEMBER 14

No person can do everything;
but everyone can do something.

FEBRUARY 16

When someone unlocks your compassion,
you have been given an assignment from heaven.

NOVEMBER 15

Temptations will knock at your door;
don't ask them to stay for dinner.

PROVERB

FEBRUARY 15

No door is locked so tight
that the key of love can't open it.

NOVEMBER 16

He that is faithful in that which is least is faithful also in much.

LUKE 16:10

FEBRUARY 14

Beloved, let us love one another:
for love is of God.

1 JOHN 4:7

NOVEMBER 17

***

Conversation is always good,
but it's even better when shared
with friends.

FEBRUARY 13

They that trust in the LORD shall be as mount Zion,
which cannot be removed, but abideth for ever.

PSALM 125:1

NOVEMBER 18

Unto thee, O LORD, do I lift up my soul.

PSALM 25:1

FEBRUARY 12

Our hearts are linked through the love of God.

NOVEMBER 19

Give unto the LORD the glory due unto his name.

PSALM 29:2

FEBRUARY 11

If you know people who are in need,
serve them. . .minister to them!

NOVEMBER 20

To every thing there is a season,
and a time to every purpose under the heaven.

ECCLESIASTES 3:1

FEBRUARY 10

Watch and pray,
that ye enter not into temptation.

MATTHEW 26:41

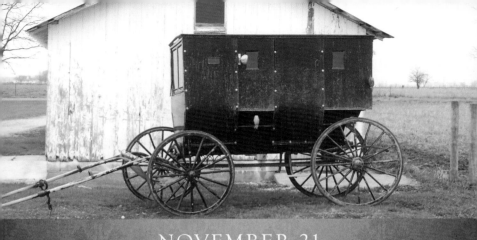

NOVEMBER 21

The secret to a happy life is being thankful
for the blessings each new day brings.

FEBRUARY 9

And let the beauty of the LORD our God be upon us.

PSALM 90:17

NOVEMBER 22

In every thing give thanks:
for this is the will of God
in Christ Jesus concerning you.

1 Thessalonians 5:18

FEBRUARY 8

God pours His love into our hearts
to flow out to the hearts of others.

NOVEMBER 23

When you have learned to be
thankful for every blessing sent,
There will be little time left for
murmur or lament.

FEBRUARY 7

God does not shield us from life's storms;
He shelters us in life's storms.

NOVEMBER 24

It's better to look ahead and prepare than
to look back and despair.
A PROVERB

FEBRUARY 6

Pray without ceasing.
1 Thessalonians 5:17

NOVEMBER 25

Be thankful not only for what you have
received but also for those things that,
by the grace of God, you have escaped.

FEBRUARY 5

Find contentment in enjoying life—
right where you are—
today, instead of always dreaming
about what's next.

NOVEMBER 26

Contentment is not possessing everything,
but giving thanks for everything you possess.

UNKNOWN

FEBRUARY 4

God's love fills our days with radiant light.

NOVEMBER 27

Prosperity is having enough to complete
God's plans for your life.

FEBRUARY 3

Be still, and know that I am God.
PSALM 46:10

NOVEMBER 28

I want to remember to praise God for everything.
No matter if I'm glad or sad, His praises I will sing.
I want to remember to worship Him all of my days,
To read God's Holy Bible and offer my heartfelt praise.

FEBRUARY 2

Commitment is a final decision
to meet the needs of the people
God has called you to serve.

NOVEMBER 29

A man seldom knows what
he is capable of until he tries to undo
what he has already done.

FEBRUARY 1

If we love one another,
God dwelleth in us,
and his love is perfected in us.

1 JOHN 4:12

NOVEMBER 30

If you just take the time to look,
you'll find that there are miracles all around.

JANUARY 31

The hand of the heavenly Father
is in all good things.

DECEMBER 1

Make the most of today—and make it beautiful.

JANUARY 30

Heavenly Father, help me to know that
You are in control,
and fill me with Your perfect peace.
Please give me a heart of acceptance.
Amen.

DECEMBER 2

For how great is his goodness,
and how great is his beauty!

ZECHARIAH 9:17

JANUARY 29

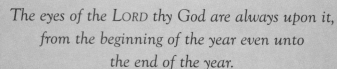

*The eyes of the LORD thy God are always upon it,
from the beginning of the year even unto
the end of the year.*

DEUTERONOMY 11:12

DECEMBER 3

Heavenly Father, how I love singing praises to You!

JANUARY 28

With God's help, you can become the
wonderful person He had in mind when He created you.

DECEMBER 4

Isn't it reassuring to know
that God never requires us
to stand on our own strength?

JANUARY 27

An attitude of acceptance
Gives one a sense of peace.
When we trust God to know
what's best for us,
Our anxiety and tension will cease.

DECEMBER 5

* • ✦ • * • ✦ • * • ✦ • *

From the rising of the sun
unto the going down of the same
the LORD's *name is to be praised.*

PSALM 113:3

JANUARY 26

For the things which are seen are temporal;
but the things which are not seen are eternal.

2 CORINTHIANS 4:18

DECEMBER 6

Choosing to follow Christ is
the right decision—every time!

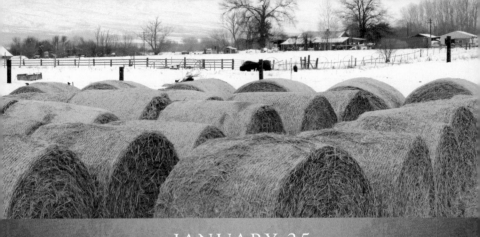

JANUARY 25

Your attitude often determines the seasons of your life.

DECEMBER 7

Driving in the wrong direction will never
get you to the right destination.

JANUARY 24

❖━━❖━━❖

Heavenly Father, remind me often
to wear the clothes of humility.
May others see You living in me. *Amen.*

DECEMBER 8

Nature is filled with beautiful signs,
all pointing to the Creator.

JANUARY 23

*For I have learned,
in whatsoever state I am,
therewith to be content.*

PHILIPPIANS 4:11

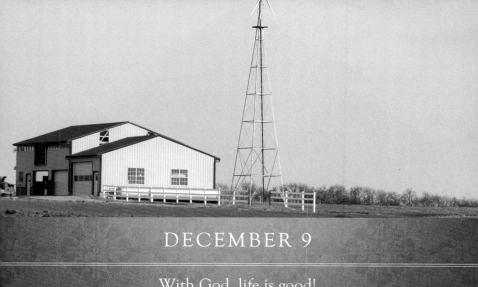

DECEMBER 9

With God, life is good!

JANUARY 22

By this shall all men know that ye are my disciples,
if ye have love one to another.
John 13:35

DECEMBER 10

Do what you can, and trust that God
will take care of the rest.

JANUARY 21

Let your light so shine before men,
that they may see your good works,
and glorify your Father which is in heaven.

MATTHEW 5:16

DECEMBER 11

The entrance of thy words giveth light;
it giveth understanding unto the simple.

PSALM 119:130

JANUARY 20

Instead of trying to influence
people with your words,
let them see your spirit shine for the Lord.

DECEMBER 12

God's Word will light even the darkest path.

JANUARY 19

Keep looking up;
for God is looking down.

DECEMBER 13

He hath made every thing beautiful in his time.

ECCLESIASTES 3:11

JANUARY 18

- - - ● - - - ● - - - ● - - -

Lord, help me to have a humble attitude,
Not prideful, conceited, or vain.
I want to be an example to others,
Never haughty, just humble and plain.

DECEMBER 14

For by him were all things created,
that are in heaven, and that are in earth.

COLOSSIANS 1:16

JANUARY 17

When you have the heavenly Father on your side,
nothing is ever as difficult as it first appears.

DECEMBER 15

Even, and especially, in our human weakness,
God will show His power and might.

JANUARY 16

Instead of clinging to fear,
try trusting God!

DECEMBER 16

Keep your eyes on the Lord;
you'll never lose sight of your purpose.

JANUARY 15

*I will say of the LORD,
He is my refuge and my fortress: my God;
in him will I trust.*

PSALM 91:2

DECEMBER 17

Seeking God's plan for your life
will always grow your faith.

JANUARY 14

Fear thou not; for I am with thee:
be not dismayed; for I am thy God.

Isaiah 41:10

DECEMBER 18

Read God's Word and spend time in His presence;
He will take your worries away.

JANUARY 13

Be at peace!
God never sleeps.

DECEMBER 19

Serve the LORD with gladness:
come before his presence with singing.

PSALM 100:2

JANUARY 12

You can't speak a kind word too soon.

DECEMBER 20

The spirit of God hath made me,
and the breath of the Almighty hath
given me life.

JOB 33:4

JANUARY 11

There is nothing as sweet as fellowship
with other believers.

DECEMBER 21

The God who sustains the universe sustains me.
UNKNOWN

JANUARY 10

Conversion takes only a moment;
transformation, a lifetime.

DECEMBER 22

Stamp God's Word on your heart;
it will keep you from losing your way.

JANUARY 9

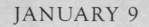

Good friends are like good quilts;
they never lose their warmth.

A Proverb

DECEMBER 23

There's nothing quite so special
As spending time with those I love.
I'm sure God is pleased
As He looks down from above.

JANUARY 8

Even the most wonderful pleasures
of earth cannot be compared to the
glorious joys of heaven.

DECEMBER 24

Keep your focus on Christ—
everything else in life will come into proper perspective.

JANUARY 7

Wash me, and I shall be whiter than snow.
PSALM 51:7

DECEMBER 25

The evidence of God's presence far
outweighs the proof of His absence.

UNKNOWN

JANUARY 6

Even the moon and the
sun obey God's will.

DECEMBER 26

──•◆•──────•◆•──────•◆•──

My meditation of him shall be sweet:
I will be glad in the LORD.

PSALM 104:34

JANUARY 5

God is light, and in him is no darkness at all.

1 JOHN 1:5

DECEMBER 27

Today, sing praises to honor the King!

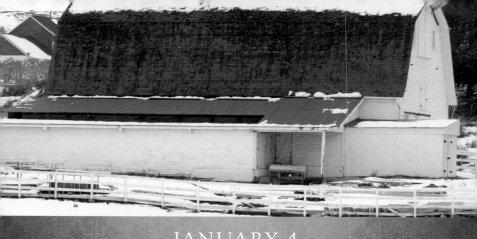

JANUARY 4

Never worry about what will happen tomorrow. . .
next week. . .next month. . .next year.
You can always trust the One who holds the future.

DECEMBER 28

Knowing God can use all things
for His good is more than enough reason
for us to give thanks in everything.

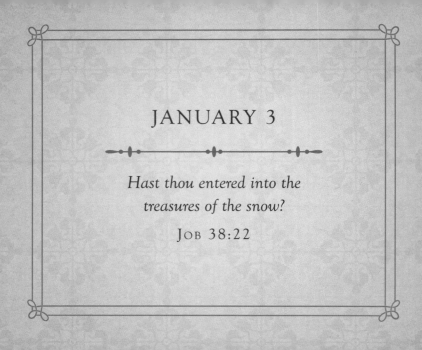

JANUARY 3

*Hast thou entered into the
treasures of the snow?*

JOB 38:22

DECEMBER 29

The glory of every morning is that it
offers us a chance to begin anew.

JANUARY 2

God is never in a hurry,
but He's always right on time.

DECEMBER 30

Keep praising God, from whom all blessings flow.

JANUARY 1

The best thing about the future is that
it comes one day at a time.

DECEMBER 31

If you're looking to make a new start,
ask God to change your heart.